UNDERSTANDING PENSIONS

THE FRIENDLY GUIDE TO PENSION SCHEMES

By Paul Kenny, B Comm., FPMI, FIIPM

Published by the Retirement Planning Council of Ireland
and
The Irish Association of Pension Funds

Dublin 1994

FOREWORD BY THE
MINISTER FOR SOCIAL WELFARE

Occupational pensions play a very important part in supplementing social welfare pensions and providing a higher standard of living for people in retirement.

At the end of 1993, we had almost 34,000 pension schemes with approximately 450,000 members. Many of these members have dependents who have a vital interest in the pension scheme. With the asset value of pension funds worth over £13bn in 1993, the well-being of pension schemes is of crucial importance to members, their families, their employers and the economy.

The Pensions Act which I introduced in 1990 was the first major piece of comprehensive legislation to provide for the regulation of occupational pension scheme and the safeguarding of members' rights and interests. The Pension Board is charged under the Act with ensuring that schemes are properly administered and that the rights of members and their dependents are safeguard.

Essentially, the Act deals with the security of pension schemes in the members' interest. It provides for matters such as duties and responsibilities of Trustees, the funding standards for schemes, equal treatment of men and women members and the preservation of benefits for members who leave early. It also provides for the disclosure to members and other interested parties of a whole range of financial and other information and gives members a say in the selection of the trustees who are responsible for administering the schemes.

It is, therefore, very important that members of schemes and prospective members are well informed about the operation of occupational pension schemes and their entitlements to information about them. For these reasons I am particularly happy to endorse publication of this book - "Understanding Pensions".

Information and good communication are vital to the success of the Pensions Act. This user-friendly publication will prove to be a valuable addition to the series of publications of members, prospective members, and their dependents.

I congratulate the Retirement Planning Council of Ireland and the Irish Association of Pension Funds on their initiative in producing this book. I also congratulate the author, Paul Kenny, for the clarity and thoroughness of his work and the Pension Board for their assistance in the project. The book is a well researched and helpful guide for those who want to know about and understand their pension schemes and their entitlements.

I wish the publication every success.

Michael Woods,
T.D. Minister for Social Welfare

ACKNOWLEDGEMENTS

I wish to thank the Minister for Social Welfare for the great interest which he has shown in this project.

My particular thanks go to the members of the co-publishers' project group who worked so hard to make this book happen - Rosalind Briggs, Camilla McAleese and Paul O'Faherty of the IAPF; Hilary Shannon, Noel O'Sullivan and Louis Slater of the Retirement Planning Council. To Louis, in particular, grateful acknowledgement is due for the help, encouragement and wise counsel which he brought to the project. I would also like to acknowledge the part played in the project by the Pensions Board, and in particular by Mary Hutch. I am especially grateful to Maria Norton, who patiently typed the numerous drafts of this book.

Finally, I must record the unique contribution of Noel O'Sullivian - not just as an active and concerned member of the project group, but because the original idea of this book was his.

PAUL KENNY
March 1994

CONTENTS

Introduction 1

A. **Questions About Your Benefits**

Section A1: Defined Benefit Schemes 5

Section A2: Defined Contribution Schemes 19

Section A3: Additional Voluntary Contributions............26

Section A4: Maximum Benefits Approvable
by the Revenue Commissioners 32

Section A5: Public Sector Pension Schemes...................39

Section A6: Public Service Transfer Networks 45

B. **Glossary of Pensions Terminology**

Section B1: Occupational Pension Schemes...................47

Section B2: Public Sector Pension Schemes...................67

Appendix: Abbreviations commonly found in
connection with pension schemes..............70

INTRODUCTION

With people now living longer than in the past, employees today need to plan for a retirement period of perhaps twenty years or more - that could be more than half as long as their total working careers. It is essential, therefore, that adequate provision should be made while working to ensure financial protection through what may be a lengthy period in retirement.

Through the State social insurance (Social Welfare) system most employees will build up entitlement to a basic pension. However, in many cases there will be need for additional pension cover if the standard of living enjoyed while at work is to be maintained into retirement.

This additional cover is provided through occupational pension schemes. These schemes enable employees and their employers to set aside, in a tax-efficient manner, a proportion of earnings in each working year to provide benefits in the form of retirement pensions and also financial protection for spouses and other dependants on a scheme member's death.

Occupational pension schemes are almost always set up as trusts. This is a requirement for approval by the tax authorities. Approval means that contributions can be deducted from an employee's pay before it is taxed and that no tax is charged on investment income earned by the scheme. The use of a trust also ensures a high measure of security for benefits due to members - scheme assets are legally separated from those of the employer. It is the responsibility of the trustees to invest the joint contributions of employees and the employer in a prudent and balanced manner and to hold and manage the accumulating assets for the benefit of scheme members and their dependants.

Most people don't appreciate that the pension rights being built up year by year by members of occupational pension schemes are probably their most valuable assets, in many cases even more valuable than a house. If you have occupational pension cover, therefore, it is most important that you should understand how your scheme works and what your entitlements are and that you keep a careful eye on how your rights are being protected.

The 1990 Pensions Act was introduced to improve and protect the rights of occupational pension scheme members and to ensure that schemes are properly controlled and administered. An important feature of the Act is that it gives members the right to obtain comprehensive knowledge of their scheme. Trustees must account to scheme members through giving them basic information about the scheme, their personal entitlements and how the scheme is being administered.

It is essential that you should know what your pension entitlements will be in retirement and those of your dependants after your death. This knowledge may help you, while time is still on your side, to decide if you have adequate cover and to take corrective action, if necessary.

A lot of basic information is already available in scheme explanatory booklets and members should be familiar with and understand the contents of these useful publications. This material will now be supplemented by a further range of data available either automatically or on request. However, there could be a difficulty for some readers in fully understanding the content of the various papers and reports because most pensions documents contain technical terms which may not be familiar to the lay person.

The purpose of this book is to endeavour to make sense of pensions – to plot a way for scheme members through what has been termed "the pensions maze". This is done through addressing the questions most often asked by members about their benefits and by supplementing the answers with glossaries of pension terms, together with separate sections relating to additional voluntary contributions (AVCs), limits imposed on benefits and contributions by the Revenue Commissioners and public sector arrangements.

For ease of reference, questions have been divided into two sections:

1. Those applicable to **defined benefit schemes,** in which the pension and other benefits which will be paid to the member and/or the member's dependants are clearly stated.

2. **Defined contribution schemes,** where the principal benefits

2

depend on the amount of contributions made and the returns earned from investing these contributions. Items which are common to both are dealt with under the "defined benefit" heading and an appropriate reference made in the other section.

It should be understood that answers, for obvious reasons, are of a general nature and cannot possibly cover every scheme as the rules of all schemes differ in one respect or another. **They should, however, enable scheme members to ask their trustees or pension scheme administrator the questions needed to enable them to get precise information about their benefits.**

While this book is designed to provide the answers to most of the questions which arise from time to time on pensions, it is recommended that it should be read in conjunction with two other publications - *What do you know about your Pension Scheme?* and *Is my Pension Secure?* - which are available free of charge from the Pensions Board, Holbrook House, 676622 Holles Street, Dublin 2.

A. QUESTIONS ABOUT YOUR BENEFITS

The main purpose of this book is to address the questions most often asked by members about their pension benefits. As stated in the introduction, answers will be of a general nature and cannot possibly cover every scheme as the rules of all schemes are different. It is essential that you get specific information before you decide on any course of action or on any option which you may be entitled to exercise. In particular, you should not take any action, defer any action, agree to exercise any option or fail to exercise it solely on the basis of information contained in this book. You should always ask your scheme trustees or administrators for any information or explanation you need in order to come to a decision. In general trust law and under the Regulations governing disclosure of information to scheme members under the Pensions Act, you are entitled to that information.

Section A1:
DEFINED BENEFIT SCHEMES

QUESTION 1.1:
At what age is normal retirement pension payable?

Normal retirement age under the rules of each scheme is the age at which the benefits specified by the rules will be paid in full. If retirement takes place before that age, a smaller benefit would usually be payable. Conversely, if late retirement is allowed, most schemes would provide a larger benefit.

"Normal Retirement Age" in most Irish pension schemes is 65, because this is the age at which the social welfare system pays pensions to qualified employees.

QUESTION 1.2:
How is my pension calculated?

In defined benefit schemes, pension is calculated usually by reference to a member's final pensionable pay and pensionable service. In most schemes, these two factors would be multiplied by a "pension fraction" to arrive at the member's entitlement. An example of this would be as follows:-

Pensionable Pay:	£12,000 per year
Pensionable Service:	40 years
Pension Fraction:	1/60th
Pension Entitlement:	£12,000 x 40/60 = £8,000

The following should be noted:-

Pensionable service

This will be defined in the rules of the scheme. It may be service as an employee, or service as a member of the scheme. It may be expressed in complete years, years and months or even years and days.

Pensionable Salary

This is the part of your salary which is taken into account for pension purposes. It could be your gross annual pay but is usually something lower than that. The usual starting point for calculating this is basic salary. If the scheme is "integrated" for social welfare benefits (see below), pensionable salary may be subject to a deduction. Anything included in pensionable pay must be taxable under Schedule E of the tax code and the Revenue Commissioners require that anything which is not a fixed part of pay (such as bonuses, commissions, etc) must be averaged over 3 years, or any shorter period for which it has actually been paid. What is included in pensionable salary in your case will depend upon the rules of your own scheme.

Final Pensionable Salary

This will be based on your pensionable salary (see above). It may be that salary taken at the date of your retirement or at some date close to that, or it could be an average over several years.

How the Social Welfare Pension can influence your Occupational Pension

It is common in Irish pension schemes that the benefits provided under the occupational pension scheme are "integrated" with the benefits paid under the Social Welfare system. In the public sector, this is known as "co-ordination". This can be done in a number of different ways. Sometimes it is done simply by subtracting all or part of the amount of the single person's Social Welfare retirement pension from the pension calculated on the scale or the formula contained in the rules of the scheme. Most commonly, however, it is done by means of a salary "offset". This works by reducing the salary for pension purposes by an amount which is related to the Social Welfare pension currently payable. Members' benefits and contributions would then be based on this lower pensionable salary. The thinking behind this is that the Social Welfare pension is considered to cater for a person's pension needs in relation to that part of salary, and only the balance needs to be provided under the occupational pension scheme.

QUESTION 1.3:

Can I receive a cash payment instead of part of my pension?

In most pension schemes, the answer is "yes". The term *commutation* is used to indicate the right, which members usually have under pension scheme rules, to exchange part of their pension for a lump sum. This lump sum is payable tax free (unlike the part of your pension that you exchange for it). The lump sum paid by any pension scheme will usually be based on the final pensionable salary and pensionable service of a member and the maximum allowed by the Revenue Commissioners is 1.5 times final pay. Exactly what is payable as a tax free lump sum depends upon the rules of your own scheme. One way or the other, the maximum benefit cannot be paid to anyone who has less than 20 years service at normal retirement age. The Revenue Commissioners require smaller amounts to apply to shorter service, and to early retirement. The rate at which the lump sum is then converted into equivalent pension will also vary from scheme to scheme. The most common formula in Ireland is probably £900 cash = £100 annual pension.

In public sector schemes, lump sums are not given by commutation, but are provided separately from each member's pension entitlement.

QUESTION 1.4:

How are pension scheme benefits taxed?

In Ireland, schemes which have "exempt" approval from the Revenue Commissioners don't pay tax on their investment income. When benefits come to be paid, however, they may be taxable.

Retirement Benefits

Benefits payable in lump sum form on retirement (up to certain limits – see Question 1.3) are not subject to income tax. Benefits payable in pension form are taxed under the PAYE system, just like salary. However, they don't attract full PRSI contributions, but only the Health Contribution and the Employment and Training Levy. This is PRSI Class K1.

Death Benefits

Similarly, benefits which are allowed to be paid in lump sum form on the death of a member are not subject to income tax, but those paid in pension form are taxable under PAYE. [See Question 1.12].

Foreign Benefits

If you have pension benefits payable from a foreign country, the tax treatment of these benefits when you receive them will vary. In some cases, they will already have been subject to foreign tax and you may be able to get credit for this against your own tax liability here. Benefits payable from the United Kingdom can be exempted from U.K. tax but you must make proper application for this to be done. In all cases where foreign pensions are payable, you should check with your local tax office.

Death benefits can be subject to Inheritance Tax [see Question 1.12].

QUESTION 1.5:

Do pensions increase after retirement?

Where payment of increases in pensions after they start to be paid is provided for in the scheme rules, this is often called "escalation". Some schemes do not provide any such increases. Where increases are provided, the amount of the increase is often a defined percentage figure, or may be related to a suitable index, such as the Consumer Price Index. In some schemes, increases are provided purely at the trustees' discretion and this usually happens where no specific funding is being made in advance for pension increases.

Sometimes increases in pensions are paid, not from the pension fund, but purely from the income of the employer. In this case, these increases would be likely to cease if the employer closed down.

In many Public Sector schemes, it is customary for pensions to be increased in line with any changes which take place in the salary appropriate to the post formerly held by a retired member.

QUESTION 1.6:

How soon may I retire?

Retirement before normal retirement age is usually subject to the consent of the employer and/or the trustees. The Revenue Commissioners will permit a pension to be paid at any age if it is due to ill-health. Otherwise, the minimum age at which a person can receive a pension is normally age 50. A member who retires in advance of normal pension age could expect a reduction in pension benefits and this reduction can be quite large if the period from the date of retirement to normal pension age is long.

The reduction takes place because

■ Fewer contributions have been paid and those which have been paid have been invested for a shorter time;

■ The payment of the pension starts earlier, the average expectation of life is longer, leading to a longer period of payment of benefits.

If early retirement takes place due to ill-health, sometimes a scheme will give better benefits than would be paid on early retirement in normal health.

Please note that the rules of each scheme will specify the earliest date at which retirement will be allowed under that scheme.

QUESTION 1.7:

What happens if I retire late?

If your retirement is to be postponed beyond normal retirement age, this usually requires the consent of your employer and/or the trustees of the scheme.

What happens then depends very much on the rules of the individual scheme. Revenue rules, and the provisions of most pension schemes, give the option to take all of your benefits at normal retirement age.

Alternatively, you may have an option to take the cash element (see Question 1.3 above) and defer receiving your pension until you actually do retire. The third option is to defer your benefits altogether until you eventually retire. If that option is taken, death in service cover may continue to be provided until you actually retire, although it would be unusual for this provision to continue after age 70.

If you defer your benefits beyond normal retirement age, it is usual for these benefits to increase, to reflect the fact that their value continues to be invested in the fund, and that average life expectancy will be shorter from a later age, so fewer instalments of pension will be payable overall.

QUESTION 1.8:

I have contributed for 40 years but I have not yet reached normal retirement age. Can I stop my contributions, or even retire now on full benefits?

The answer to the first question depends very much on the rules of your scheme. Some schemes will permit members to stop contributing after 40 years of contributions but most schemes require people to continue to contribute up to normal pension age, even if this means that they would have contributed for longer than the maximum period of service credited for pension purposes.

If you want to take your benefits before the normal retirement age specified in the scheme rules, this is a case of early retirement and your benefits in those circumstances would be subject to whatever reduction the scheme would usually require for benefits paid before normal retirement age.

QUESTION 1.9:

What happens if I die before retirement age?

Almost all pension schemes provide some sort of death in service benefit designed to provide for the dependants of members who die before reaching pension age. These death in service benefits take the following forms:-

(i) Lump Sum Benefits

These are payable income tax-free and are often expressed as a multiple of salary. The maximum lump sum benefit which the Revenue Commissioners will allow is four times your final pay. However, your own contributions **can** be refunded in lump sum form in addition, with or without interest. This refund of contributions would also be tax free. If the benefit provided in the form of a capital sum exceeds the Revenue limits on cash payments, anything over the limits must be used to provide a pension for a dependant or other beneficiary. Check the rules of your own scheme.

(ii) Pensions for Dependants

Many schemes provide pensions for dependants in addition to lump sum benefits. These pensions can take the form of spouses' benefits, spouses' and children's benefits, or benefits payable to dependants generally. The amount of these pensions is regulated by the Revenue Commissioners and the total cannot exceed the maximum pension which you could have had, based on your final pay and the service you would have completed had you lived to normal retirement age.

(iii) Preserved Benefits

If you have left employment since the 1st January 1993 **and** are entitled to preserved benefits under the Pensions Act, the value of these benefits must be paid to your estate in the event of your death. Alternatively, the trustees of your Pension Scheme may have chosen the option to pay a dependant's pension instead. The notification of your benefits on leaving service will specify what is payable in the event of your death, and in what manner it may be paid.

(iv) Death in Retirement

Benefits payable after the death of a pensioner in retirement vary considerably from scheme to scheme. It is quite unusual for any benefit to be paid *in lump sum form* when death occurs more than 5 years after retirement. See Question 1.10.

Beneficiaries may be liable to Inheritance Tax on these benefits. See Question 1.12.

What happens if I die after retirement?

Death in retirement benefits can be any one or more of the following:-

Guarantee

Many pension schemes provide a guaranteed minimum period for payment of your benefits, whether you live or die. This can be up to 10 years. However, if it is 5 years or less, then the remaining instalments payable under this guarantee can be translated on your death into a lump sum payable to your dependants or estate instead. If the guarantee is more than 5 years, the outstanding instalments must be taken in pension form.

Dependants' benefits provided by surrender

Many pension schemes give a retiring employee the option to give up some personal pension in order to provide for a continuing pension to be paid to a dependant on death after retirement. This is an option which has to be exercised before you actually retire. The cost to you in terms of a reduction in your own benefits will depend on the age and sex of your dependant, relative to your own age and sex. The older the dependant, the less of your own pension you will have to give up to make this sort of provision.

Dependants' Pensions

Sometimes the scheme rules will provide for specific dependants' pensions to be paid on your death after retirement, without any need for you to give up part of your own pension. These benefits may be payable immediately on the death of a pensioner, even though a 5 year guarantee might still be in force, or they may begin payment after the guarantee expires.

Marriage after Retirement

Generally speaking, pension schemes which provide spouses' pensions on death after retirement cater only for the spouse to which the pensioner was married at the time retirement took place. The same usually applies in the case of other nominated dependants - payment will be confined to the dependant/s nominated at the point of retirement. However, you should check the rules of your own scheme for precise information in this area.

QUESTION 1.11:

Who gets my death benefits?

The rules of the majority of pension schemes specify that the lump sum death in service benefits are payable to a broad category of "dependants". These will normally include a member's wife or husband and children under 18. Often, in addition, the category of dependants will include those over 18 who are still receiving education or who are mentally or physically handicapped, and any person who was ordinarily dependent on the member for the necessaries of life. Remember, the definition of dependants can vary considerably from scheme to scheme and you should check your scheme booklet or other explanatory documents.

Discretionary Powers of Trustees

In most schemes, the trustees will have a fairly wide discretion to decide who gets these benefits. In some schemes, apart from "dependants" as outlined above, there might also be a broader category of eligible beneficiaries whom the trustees can choose to pay. You cannot direct the trustees in the way they exercise these discretionary powers (but see next paragraph).

Nomination of Dependants

The trustees may give you the option of completing a form of nomination of dependants, often known as a "wishes letter" or "expression of wishes". The purpose of this is to specify your own wishes in the disposal of your death benefit. Such a letter or expression of wishes cannot bind the trustees but they will normally try to give effect to your wishes. They will not do so, however, where your wishes are in conflict with the obligations imposed by law on trustees.

Spouses' Pensions

If the dependants' pensions are expressed as "spouses' pensions" in the scheme rules, they can be paid only to the lawful spouse of the member.

Payment to the estate

The majority of pension schemes do not provide for payment of your death benefit to your estate except, perhaps, where there are no dependants. However, the Pensions Act does require the value of any compulsory Preserved Benefits under that Act to be paid to your estate. Any amount paid to your estate will be disposed of in accordance with your will, or in accordance with the rules on intestacy if you don't make a will. Every pension scheme member should make a will.

Leaving Death Benefits by will:

You can leave you death benefits to someone else by means of your will **only** if the death benefit is paid into your estate. In most pension schemes, this does not happen immediately, because the death benefits are usually expressed as something payable to dependants. Generally, payment to your estate will take place only if you have no dependants (except in the case of preserved benefits as mentioned in the previous paragraph). Therefore, in most cases, your will would have absolutely no effect on who becomes entitled to the benefits payable under the rules of the pension scheme on your death. You should also note that benefits payable to dependants or other beneficiaries under the rules of the scheme can be paid fairly quickly after the death of the scheme member. Benefits which have to be paid to the estate could not be paid until the estate has been granted probate (or until letters of administration have been granted, if there is no will).

QUESTION 1.12:

How are my death benefits treated for tax purposes?

As has already been stated (see question 1.4) benefits are taken into account for tax only when they come into payment. Any benefits which the Revenue Commissioners allow to be paid as lump sums in normal circumstances are not taxed. Benefits payable in pension form are subject to tax under the PAYE system, so the tax payable on them will be determined by the individual tax position of whoever is receiving the payment.

There is another tax to which death benefits can be exposed. Benefits paid on death are regarded as part of your estate for the purposes of Inheritance Tax, even though you cannot normally control who gets these benefits by means of your will.

For the purposes of inheritance tax, death benefits are treated like every other inheritance. The amount of tax payable (if any) depends on who is receiving the benefit and their relationship to you. For example, if the only beneficiary is your husband or wife, no inheritance tax would be payable. If a child or children receive the benefit, anything they get from the pension scheme will be added to whatever else they have inherited for the purpose of calculating whether they are liable to tax or not. The thresholds for relatives other than children are low and, for non-relatives, even lower still. In summary, therefore, if your death benefit is inherited by anyone except your lawful spouse, there is at least a possibility that inheritance tax will be payable. Non-relatives, such as a dependant who is not legally married to you, are the most likely people to pay substantial amounts of inheritance tax. The trustees will want to satisfy themselves that the liability for inheritance tax has been taken care of before they pay out the full death benefit, as they could be held liable for payment of the tax otherwise. Pension scheme benefits are not subject to the probate tax introduced in 1993.

QUESTION 1.13:

What are my options on leaving service?

Under the Pensions Act, your pension scheme trustees have an obligation to let you have a detailed note of the full options available to you on leaving service. The following may help you to understand what these options mean:-

(a)   What are vested rights?

This is a term used to describe a right which a pension scheme member acquires to a benefit on leaving service. This is provided for in the rules of the scheme. It may apply automatically on leaving service, usually after a certain minimum period of service, regardless of the circumstances in which you leave. It is quite common for vested rights to apply only if you leave through no fault of your own, such as through redundancy. Vested rights should not be confused with the right to **preserved benefits** under the Pensions Act.

(b) What are preserved benefits?

Preserved benefits are benefits "earned" during service as a member of a pension scheme after the 1st January 1991, the date on which the Pensions Act came into operation. They are available to those who leave service after the 1st January 1993, and who have been at least 5 years in the pension scheme, in any other scheme of the same employer or in any pension scheme from which rights have been transferred to your present scheme. In defined benefit schemes, these benefits will be subject to "revaluation" (see Section B1) between 1996 (or later date of leaving service) and the time you collect your benefits.

(c) What is a transfer value?

This term is explained in the glossary in Section B1.

(d) Can I take a refund of contributions made to the scheme by
(i) myself and
(ii) my employer?

If you are entitled to a preserved benefit (see above) under the Pensions Act, your right to take a refund of your own contributions will now be limited to those contributions made before the 31st December 1990. This also applies to voluntary contributions. If, however, you have not completed enough service to acquire rights to a preserved pension, you can take a refund of all your own contributions, subject to whatever the rules of your scheme provide. Interest may or may not be payable, depending on the detailed rules of your own scheme. The tax currently payable on a refund of contributions is 25%.

You can **never** take a refund of the contributions made by your employer to the scheme on leaving service.

Will a transfer value buy an equivalent period of service in a new scheme?

In general terms, the answer to this is "no". It is usually up to the trustees of the receiving scheme to decide what credit you are given in the new scheme in return for any transfer value paid in. This decision will generally be made on the advice of the scheme actuary. No two schemes are the same in every detail but, even if they were, the benefits which you take from the first scheme are likely to be calculated on your pay at the time you leave service, not on the pay you will be receiving when you retire from the service of the second employer. If you are considering asking for a transfer payment, you should obtain detailed information on what it is likely to buy for you in the new scheme before you ask for the money to be transferred. If the transfer value will not replace all of your service, you may be able to make up some or all of the difference by making Additional Voluntary Contributions (AVCs). See Section A3.

(a) How are my personal contributions calculated?

The rules of your scheme will contain a formula, normally expressing your contributions as a percentage of pensionable salary. If your scheme is "integrated" with social welfare, you may have a pensionable salary which is lower than your actual salary. (See the explanations of these terms in the glossary). If your pensionable salary is calculated by subtracting from your basic salary in order to arrive at your pay for pension purposes, the contribution which you pay would be based on the adjusted figure. Sometimes earnings other than basic pay may also be counted for pension purposes. Only the detailed rules of your own scheme will provide an accurate answer to this question.

(b) Is there tax relief on contributions?

Yes. Contributions which you make, including additional voluntary contributions, up to a maximum limit of 15% of your gross earnings, will receive income tax relief. The relief will be given at your marginal rate of tax and, since contributions are normally deducted from your pay before tax is calculated, you will also receive relief from PRSI on these contributions. However, the maximum allowable contribution by you is subject to the condition that the employer must, overall, have paid at least 1/6th of the total cost of your benefits. In other words, tax relief would not be available on a scheme which was funded solely by contributions from members.

QUESTION 1.16:

Have I got scope for Additional Voluntary Contributions?

Whether or not you have scope for additional voluntary contributions will depend on the extent to which there is a gap between the maximum benefits permitted by the Revenue Commissioners and the benefits actually being provided in the scheme. The scope for additional voluntary contributions generally arises where:-

(i) not all pay is pensioned. For example, if your scheme is "integrated" with social welfare or if you have non-pensioned pay, such as overtime, bonuses or benefits in kind.

(ii) the scheme does not provide for the absolute maximum benefit which the Revenue would approve.

The scope to make voluntary contributions may be limited by the amount of your employer's contributions to the scheme (see 1.15 (b)) and by having to take *retained benefits* (see Section B1) into account.

You should be aware that you cannot make voluntary contributions at all unless the rules of the pension scheme permit this, or there is a separate scheme in existence designed to cater for them.

Section A2:
DEFINED CONTRIBUTION SCHEMES

QUESTION 2.1:
At what age is normal retirement pension payable?

Normal retirement age is exactly the same under defined contribution schemes as it is under Defined Benefit Schemes (see question 1.1).

QUESTION 2.2:
How does a defined contribution scheme work?

Unlike a Defined Benefit Scheme, where the rules promise you a specific benefit on retirement at normal retirement age, a defined contribution scheme does not make such a promise. Instead, what you are promised is a fund which is made up of the proceeds of the investment of contributions paid on your behalf by your employer, together with whatever contributions you make yourself. All of the contributions, plus whatever they earn, make up the assets of this fund. Such a fund does not pay any tax on its income and, when you come to retirement age, it provides a capital sum which the trustees will use to provide your benefits. The guaranteed contribution which the employer will pay on your behalf (the "defined contribution") may, or may not, include the cost of death benefit. Sometimes this is paid for in addition to a defined pension contribution; in other cases, your death benefit is a first charge against the total contribution being made.

Sometimes, the overall payment being made by the employer will also include premiums payable under a Permanent Health Insurance scheme designed to give benefits in the event of prolonged disability. **This is not a part of the pension scheme and is not the responsibility of its trustees.**

At retirement, under a defined contribution scheme, you have a great deal of flexibility in planning your retirement benefits. Subject to Revenue limits (which govern the maximum amount that you can receive in cash, for example), the choice as to what you take in cash, what you take as personal pension benefits and what is provided by way of dependants' benefits on death after retirement is up to you to decide.

19

QUESTION 2.3:
How are defined contributions schemes financed?

Generally speaking, the first step in the financing of a defined contribution scheme is to fix the amount of the employer's contribution. As stated above, this might be fixed to include the cost of death benefits. Then the question of any agreed level of contribution from employees must be considered. Employers' and employees' agreed contributions will be the core payments to the defined contribution scheme. Members may make additional voluntary contributions (AVCs) on top of this.

The contributions are invested, usually in insurance contracts or unit trusts. Occasionally, they may be invested in a directly invested fund. Whichever investment medium is chosen, the contributions appropriate to each member are individually "tracked", which means that the capital sum appropriate to each person can be easily identified at any time during their membership of the scheme, and at retirement age.

QUESTION 2.4:
Can I cash in part of my pension?

Yes. The rules applying to benefits payable in lump sum form are exactly the same under defined contribution schemes as under defined benefit schemes (see question 1.3). In a defined contribution scheme, you are dealing with a capital sum and, once the amount of your cash benefit is ascertained, the balance of the capital sum must then be used to provide an annuity or annuities for yourself and possibly for your dependants. For an explanation of "annuity", see Question 2.5 below and Section B1.

QUESTION 2.5:
What are my choices when it comes to buying an annuity?

In a defined contribution scheme the choice can be very wide indeed. Where benefits are payable in pension form, there is really no choice but to purchase an annuity. Usually, regardless of where the capital fund has been built up, there will be an "open market" option, which means that the fund can be taken to any insurance company so that you can obtain the benefit of the best rates available on the market at the time you retire.

There are various types of annuity:-

■ Single Life - this is an annuity on your own life only. It will cease to be payable when you die, except insofar as there may be a minimum guaranteed period of payment (see "guarantee" in the Question 1.10).

■ Joint Life Annuity - this means an annuity which is payable during the lifetimes of both you and another person (for example your spouse). It can be designed to be paid in full as long as one of you is alive, or it could be bought on the basis that it reduces in the event of the death of either of you.

■ Post Retirement Increases - annuities can also be bought with a built in **escalation** factor, so that you would receive automatic increases during the time the annuity is payable.

What all of this means is that you have a great deal of flexibility about the precise way in which your benefits are set up at the time you retire. They can literally be tailored to suit your own circumstances, but always subject to the overall limits imposed by the Revenue Commissioners.

Don't forget also that there are numerous providers of annuities in the market and you and the trustees of your pension scheme should take expert advice before coming to any final decisions on where the annuities are bought.

QUESTION 2.6:

I would like to aim for a particular level of pension. How can I do this in a defined contribution scheme?

It is impossible to guarantee in advance any particular level of pension from a defined contribution scheme. This is because the final capital fund available to you will depend, not only on the contributions made, but on the investment income and capital growth achieved on those contributions while they are in the pension fund. Added to that is the fact that annuity rates do fluctuate. As it would be impossible to predict these with any certainty, years in advance of your retirement, it is not possible to target very accurately the particular level of pension.

Having said that, it is possible on the basis of professional advice to arrive at an appropriate level of contribution for any particular target benefit, using assumptions in relation to investment returns and future pay increases. There will be no guarantee of reaching the target but it may be possible, over your lifetime in a pension fund, to make some corrections to the rate at which the pension is funded, in order to stay close to the target and compensate for fluctuations in investment returns. The most important thing here is that advice is needed.

QUESTION 2.7:
How are benefits taxed?

See the answer to question 1.4.

QUESTION 2.8:
Can I retire early from a defined contribution scheme?

Yes. The Revenue Commissioners' rules on early retirement apply equally to defined benefit and defined contribution schemes. However, in a defined contribution scheme, instead of having a specific benefit reduced because of early payment, you would simply have available to you whatever is the capital value of your particular share of the fund at the point of early retirement. After payment of whatever cash is appropriate, the balance would be applied to the purchase of an annuity. Don't forget, the younger you are when an annuity is bought, the smaller the annual payment is likely to be.

Subject to your scheme rules, you may take your early retirement benefits at any time due to ill-health, or after the age of 50 in other circumstances. See question 1.6.

QUESTION 2.9:
What happens if I die before retirement age?

This topic has been dealt with in detail in question 1.9 under the heading of Defined Benefits. However, there are some features which are peculiar to defined contribution schemes, as follows:-

- The lump sum death benefit may be available to the trustees as a separately insured amount, in addition to the fund of money appropriate to your retirement benefits.

- Sometimes, a lump sum death benefit may be expressed as a multiple of salary, e.g., 3 or 4 times annual pay, which may include the total fund of money which represents your retirement benefits.

- It is less usual for dependants' benefits to be provided in pension form from defined contribution schemes than it is from defined benefit schemes. Where dependants' benefits are provided in pension form, they will normally be expressed as a percentage of the salary on which contributions are based, rather than being related to your own pension entitlement. From the previous questions in this section, you will realise that your own pension entitlement is not defined and it would not therefore be possible to define a dependant's pension in terms of your own entitlement.

The rules of your own pension scheme will specify how exactly your death benefit is determined, and any limitations on the manner in which it can be paid.

QUESTION 2.10:
What happens if I die after retirement?

In defined contribution schemes there is no specific provision for payment to be made to dependants on your death after retirement. Any guaranteed period of payment of your own pension, or any dependant's pension to be paid after your death must be arranged by you at the time you retire, out of the total fund of money available for retirement provision.

QUESTION 2.11:
Who gets my death benefits?

See question 1.11.

How are my death benefits treated for tax purposes?

See question 1.12.

What are my options on leaving service?

The options that you have on leaving service are the same as those
described in questions 1.13 and 1.14.

In defined contribution schemes, the preserved benefits applicable under
the Pensions Act are defined as being the value at the date of leaving
service of the contributions paid by you and on your behalf since the 1st
January 1991.

In a defined contribution scheme, if you request a transfer value, the
trustees have power to fix the date on which the transfer value is
calculated, since the value of the investments representing your benefits
can change from day to day - it does not become fixed just because you
leave service.

What scope is there for me to pay additional contributions?

Within the general limits placed by the Revenue Commissioners on
benefits and contributions (described in Section A4) there is a good deal
of scope for a member of a defined contribution scheme to pay extra
contributions. Sometimes, defined contribution schemes are set up on the
basis of a fairly basic contribution rate from the employer. An employer
contribution rate as low as 3% would be sufficient to allow the scheme
member to make the maximum allowable contribution of 15% of salary.
See Section A3 - AVCs, also questions 1.15 (b) and 1.16.

In general, scheme members, particularly those at younger ages, who
wish to make large additional contributions, should always check that the
benefits which result from making these contributions, when added to
the benefits under the main pension scheme, are likely to be within the

overall benefit limits imposed by the Revenue Commissioners. See Section A4.

You should also note that one of the conditions imposed by the Revenue Commissioners is that the employer must meet at least 1/6th of the total cost of benefits under the scheme if the scheme is to be approved for tax purposes. This test must be met on a year-by-year basis in a defined contribution scheme.

QUESTION 2.15:

Have I any say in how my fund is invested?

This depends upon how your scheme is run by its trustees. You should bear in mind that the trustees have the ultimate legal responsibility for the investment of every pension fund but it is fair to say that it is the scheme member who carries the investment risk in a defined contribution scheme. Trustees may therefore be willing to allow each member to have some say in the investment of that part of the fund which represents his or her benefits. You do not have an automatic right to such consultation, because the legal responsibility belongs to the trustees.

Very often, trustees will give scheme members a range of options - for example, a deposit or a cash fund and some sort of mixed fund with a variety of different investments in it. The degree of risk attaching to each of these funds will be different. A deposit fund is likely to give a steady (but possibly low) rate of return. A managed fund may give returns that fluctuate widely from year to year and show no regular pattern of returns. On the other hand, over the longer term, the returns from such funds can be attractive. Usually, investments which involve low risks also involve low returns, and vice versa.

With this in mind, it is clearly not appropriate for an older person, fairly close to retirement, to invest in a fund which is likely to show very volatile returns. This approach might be appropriate for a younger person. As the member gets older, gains made from these forms of investment can be realised and consolidated into a deposit or cash fund, where at least the value of the investments is unlikely to go down, something which is always possible with investments based on stocks and shares.

This is an area where it is really impossible to generalise and detailed advice should be sought.

Section A.3:
ADDITIONAL VOLUNTARY CONTRIBUTIONS

This section of the book is intended to cover private sector arrangements for Additional Voluntary Contributions. Similar arrangements can be established alongside public sector schemes. However, this section does not cover the special "added years" provisions which are available in most public sector employments.

For ease of reference, we shall use the term "AVCs", meaning Additional Voluntary Contributions, as this is the term most frequently used to describe them. Where the main scheme is non-contributory, they cannot, strictly speaking, be called "additional" but the expression "AVC" is used for the sake of brevity.

What are AVCs?

Voluntary contributions are made by employees in addition to any compulsory contributions which they may make. AVCs are used to improve the benefits of members, over and above those provided by the scheme rules, but within Revenue limits.

How are they documented?

It is necessary for the rules of a pension scheme to make provision for AVCs if scheme members wish to make them. However, the law does not require schemes to allow AVCs. If your scheme rules do not allow them at present, you would have to get your employer's consent to change the rules in order to permit voluntary contributions. Alternatively, a separate scheme can be set up to accommodate AVCs but this, again, would need the co-operation of your employer.

Why make voluntary contributions?

AVCs can be used, within the limits imposed by the Revenue Commissioners to:-

- Increase basic pension or provide benefits based on non-pensionable pay.

- Increase tax free lump sum, if possible.

- Provide or increase dependants' provisions on death in retirement.

26

- Provide or increase cost of living provision on all benefits.

- Increase death in service provision.

- Provide additional security for you and/or your dependants if you retire early.

The presence of AVCs alongside the benefits available under the main scheme can make it attractive, or even just possible, to accept early retirement, although Revenue rules don't permit specific additional funding with a view to retiring early.

In considering the possible application of AVCs, the following questions are relevant:-

- Is all pay pensioned?

- Is the main pension scheme integrated with social welfare? If it is, the gap thus created can be catered for, in terms of increases in both basic pension and tax free cash.

- Is pensionable service short? Is all service pensionable?

- Has the employee got dependants and if so are dependants' benefits already provided, or are they adequate?

- Is there provision for cost of living increases? If so, is it adequate?

Revenue Requirements

These are dealt with under various headings in other Sections of this book but they are here summarised:-

- Total member contributions may not exceed 15% of gross pay in any tax year, inclusive of any contributions already required by the scheme rules.

- AVCs made annually should usually be deducted on a "net pay" basis. This gives immediate tax relief at the point of payment.

- Revenue approval is needed for "special" contributions, i.e. those not being made on a regular basis. Tax relief on these will be spread forward or, if this is not possible or practicable, it may be allocated to earlier tax years, subject to a maximum of 10 years.

- When the benefits secured by AVCs are added to the main scheme benefits, the maximum Revenue limits on benefits must not be exceeded.

- No employee may, by the time of retirement, have contributed more than 5/6ths of the total cost of the benefits he receives from the company pension scheme, including the AVC arrangement. This test must be met on a year-on-year basis in defined contribution schemes.

Advantages of AVCs

- Full and immediate relief from income tax, and from PRSI on contributions deducted at source.

- The fund in which the contributions are invested does not attract tax.

- AVCs give the member a facility to have some control over benefit levels, by choosing the pace of additional saving for retirement. The "mix" of benefits at the time of retirement (between personal pension, dependants' provisions, cost-of-living increases, etc.) can be adjusted to suit individual circumstances.

- Present legislation allows for the AVC fund to be paid as an additional lump sum on death.

Disadvantages of AVCs

- Contributions are locked in and may emerge only as benefits on death, retirement or leaving service and you should note that the scope for cash refunds of contributions is limited.

- Unlike life assurance policies, a voluntary contribution fund may not be assigned, charged or borrowed against and it is therefore outside the employee's effective control until it emerges as benefits.

- AVCs are not short term savings. While it is possible for a member to stop contributing, no refund of contributions is possible, except in limited circumstances on leaving employment as explained above.

- If a refund of contribution is taken on leaving service, this would usually exclude the possibility of any other benefit from the company pension scheme.

Form of AVC Scheme / Investment

In the private sector, AVCs mostly take the form of defined contributions. It is quite unusual for benefits secured by AVCs to be set up on a defined benefit basis. For this reason, the investment considerations in AVC schemes are generally the same as those for defined contribution schemes.

Your AVCs and the Main Pension Scheme

Obviously, it is important for every member considering the question of Additional Voluntary Contributions to get proper advice. This advice should take into account the benefits being provided under the main pension scheme, as well as the member's own personal circumstances and considerations such as tax relief and possible return on the fund. Remember that your employer's co-operation, at very least, is needed if you want to set up a voluntary contribution arrangement for yourself. However, bear in mind that most voluntary contribution arrangements made directly by scheme members themselves could involve the employer in becoming trustee, if these arrangements are set up outside the main company pension scheme. Employers may not wish to become trustees in these circumstances and cannot be made trustees without their consent.

It is also very important that the trustees of the main company pension scheme should be aware that people are making voluntary contributions. It is the responsibility of the trustees to "police" the Revenue limits imposed on members' benefits and it is impossible for them to do so if they do not know that members are making voluntary contributions alongside the main scheme.

■   You may not take a refund of AVCs except to the extent that a refund of your main scheme contributions for the same period is permitted. Preservation requirements under the Pensions Act may result in restrictions in this area. If a refund is taken tax is currently payable on the amount refunded at 25%.

Excess Contributions

Because the Revenue Commissioners limit the overall level of benefits with which you can be provided under a pension scheme, it follows that

29

there is a possibility that AVCs could in certain circumstances cause the total entitlements of a member to exceed these limits. If this happens, the trustees of the main pension scheme will have no option but to cut back on the benefits provided by that scheme in order to satisfy the Revenue Commissioners' requirements. Very rarely, and only in very exceptional circumstances, is it possible for excess AVCs to be refunded.

Life Assurance or AVCs?

Sometimes, people ask "Should I make voluntary contributions or take out a life assurance policy-linked savings scheme?" The question was perhaps more relevant when some form of limited tax relief was available on life assurance contracts, but this is no longer given. Nevertheless, it might be useful if the differences were summarised, since the answer to the question is that there is probably scope for both.

- Life assurance is generally suitable for shorter term saving (but not very short term).

- The member has total control over a life policy at all times.

- The member can choose the term over which the investment is made.

- The policy can be made paid up or surrendered at any time.

- The policy can be assigned to a third party and in some cases even borrowed against.

- Under current legislation, the proceeds are always tax free.

BUT There is no tax relief on premiums and no relief from PRSI.

With AVCs, the position is different:-

- There is full tax relief on contributions and relief from PRSI if deductions are made directly from pay.

- Because of tax free build-up, an AVC fund should accumulate faster than a similarly invested savings fund.

30

- No part of the amount being saved need go to provide cover in the event of death.

BUT

- No benefits may be paid until retirement, death or leaving service.
- Benefits may not be assigned to a third party or charged with any debts under any circumstances.
- If a refund of AVCs is taken on leaving service (and this will now be a restricted right because of the preservation requirements of the Pensions Act), it is necessary for ordinary contributions to be treated similarly. Deferred benefit entitlements not preserved under the Pensions Act would be lost in these circumstances.
- The Revenue limits mean that the proceeds may not always be payable in tax free form.

Section A4
MAXIMUM BENEFITS APPROVABLE BY THE REVENUE COMMISSIONERS

A brief note of the maximum benefits approvable by the Revenue Commissioners in normal circumstances is given below. These notes are for guidance only, as it is not possible to deal briefly with every case which might arise. It should be noted that augmentation of benefits beyond a pension level of 1/60th of final remuneration for each year of service, or a commutation level of 3/80ths for each year of service, requires that non-trivial benefits from previous employments may need to be taken into account. "20% Directors" also require special treatment (these are people who, alone or with other specified people, control more than 20% of the voting rights in a company).

These pages should not be used as a substitute for the Practice Notes issued by the Retirement Benefits District of the Revenue Commissioners, which must be consulted in any case of doubt.

It is also worth noting that few, if any, occupational pension schemes can afford to provide the maximum benefits which the Revenue Commissioners will approve. Individuals may receive maximum approvable benefits, particularly if they fund for them by means of additional voluntary contributions. The distribution of surplus assets on the winding up of a scheme is another reason why people might receive benefits up to the Revenue maximum limits. In practice, however, those most often affected by maximum limits are scheme members with short service.

1. Eligibility - Who may be included?

All employees of an employer participating in a pension fund, whether full time, part time, permanent or temporary can be included. Most usually, full time permanent employees are included as members but other categories of employee participate in some schemes. The important thing to remember is that only those who are taxed under Schedule E (the part of the tax code which covers workers who pay their tax under PAYE) can be included in occupational pension schemes. Agents, consultants, partners and self-employed people who are taxed under Schedule D of the tax code may not be included.

2. Scheme Documentation

Both the Revenue Commissioners and the Pensions Act require that every employee who has a right to be a member of a scheme must be given details of all its essential features.

3. Normal Pension Age:

Any time between ages 60 to 70. If Normal Pension Age is to be changed, the Retirement Benefits District of the Revenue Commissioners must be advised.

4. Pensionable and Final Pensionable Salary

These are regulated by the rules of each scheme, but the maximum benefits permitted by the Revenue Commissioners are expressed in terms of Final Remuneration.

Final remuneration:

All Schedule E income may be pensioned, but items which fluctuate from year to year (bonuses are a good example) must be averaged over 3 years or other suitable period. Final remuneration on which maximum approvable benefits can be based may be any one of the following:-

(a)   Salary in any one of the last 5 years before retirement, plus "fluctuating emoluments" suitably averaged.

(b)   The member's total pay averaged over 3 consecutive years ending not earlier than 10 years prior to retirement date.

(c)   The rate of pay at normal pension date or any point in the final year but this may be restricted in cases where special increases or promotions applied in the 3 years before retirement.

(d)   If final remuneration is based on anything other than (c), the income may be "dynamised", i.e., increased by reference to changes in the Consumer Price Index between the dates on which such remuneration applied and the point of retirement. This can be useful where a person's actual income has not kept pace with increases in cost of living (20% Directors may be restricted).

5. Pension at Normal Pension Date

In most circumstances, a pension of 1/60th of final remuneration for each year of service may be provided, ignoring any benefits arising from previous employments. Where service is less than 5 years, no more than this formula can be provided. Where service exceeds 5 years, there is a sliding scale, from 8/60ths at 6 years of service, to 40/60ths for 10 years or more. Proportionate benefits may be added for days of service.

6. Commutation (Exchange of Pension for Cash)

A basic cash amount of 3/80ths of final remuneration for each year of service can be provided. The maximum 120/80ths may be provided for any member with at least 20 years' service at normal pension date. Where service is 8 years or less, a strict basis of 3/80ths of pay per year of service applies. For more than 8 years' service, a sliding scale goes from 30/80ths for 9 years, to 120/80ths for 20 years. A trivial pension (less than £260 per annum) may always be cashed, but its cash value will in certain circumstances be subject to a small tax charge.

7. Spouses' Pensions (Death in Service or Death in Retirement)

A maximum spouse's pension of 2/3rds of the member's pension could be provided, inclusive of any retained benefits. Additional dependants' pensions can be provided to bring the total benefit to a level equal to the member's own maximum approvable pension expectation. Children's pensions, where provided, must cease when the child is no longer dependent. The same limits apply on death in service and death in retirement.

There are some restrictions on when a pension may become payable to a spouse or other dependant on a member's death after retirement. These depend on any minimum guaranteed period of payment given with the member's own pension.

Pension schemes usually provide a minimum guaranteed period of payment of the pension, whether the pensioner lives or dies. The most common guaranteed period is 5 years but a guarantee up to 10 years can be given. If the guarantee is 5 years or less, its immediate cash value could be paid out as a lump sum, tax free, on the death of the pensioner. If the period of guarantee is more than 5 years, the remaining instalments must be paid as continuing pension and therefore subject to tax. If a spouse's or other dependant's pension is payable in addition, it may begin payment immediately in the case of a 5 year guarantee, but must not commence until the end of the guaranteed period if that is more than 5 years. This condition does not apply if the spouse's or other dependant's pension has been provided by the pensioner surrendering part of his or her pension to make this provision at the time of retirement.

8. Lump Sum Benefits on Death in Service

The maximum benefit is 4 times the final remuneration at the date of death, plus member's contributions to the scheme with interest on these. Benefits from previous employments must be taken into account. Any lump sum provided in excess of these levels must be used to purchase pensions for dependants or other beneficiaries.

9. Escalation

In general, the maximum increase which may be given on a pension after retirement is the increase in the Consumer Price Index as applied to the maximum pension which the member could have received. An exception to this is that increases of 3% per annum compound may be promised and paid, regardless of the level of inflation. Employers may fund in advance for fixed rates of increase to pensions in payment, but the actual amounts payable will be restricted by the Consumer Price Index increases. In the public sector, it is common practice to give "parity", which means that pensions increase in line with pay increases for those who are still at work.

10. Early Retirement

The minimum age at which early retirement benefits can be paid to a member in normal health is 50 years. Any departure from this has to be considered on its own merits by the Revenue Commissioners. In the event of retirement due to ill-health, there is no age limit and an employee retiring in ill-health may be given benefits up to the maximum benefits which he or she could have been given at normal pension age.

In addition, an employee whose life expectancy is very short at the time of retirement may be permitted in exceptional circumstances to receive all benefits in cash form. Any proposal to use this facility must be referred to the Retirement Benefits District of the Revenue Commissioners.

11. Limitations on Early Retirement Benefits in Normal Health

The maximum pension is either:-

1/60th of final remuneration for each year of service or **N/NS x P**;

where **N** *is actual service,* **NS** *is potential service to normal pension date and* **P** *is maximum pension at normal pension date based on current salary and total potential service.*

However, this maximum is also restricted by the short service formula which applies at normal pension date.

Example:
An employee retires early, having completed 7 years out of a potential 17. The formula is 7/17 x 2/3rds = 27.45% of salary. However, an employee retiring with only 7 years' service at normal pension date could receive only 16/60ths, equal to 26.67% so this figure is the most the employee in question could be paid (see paragraph 5, above).

This restriction applies only to immediate early retirement benefits, and not to benefits whose payment is deferred to normal pension age on leaving service. Similar formulae apply to commutation of pension for cash.

12. Late Retirement

If a member remains in service after normal pension date and total service at that date is, or exceeds, 40 years, additional benefits may be provided in respect of the service completed after normal pension date, subject to an overall maximum of 45/60ths. Lump sums can be similarly increased. Alternatively, (regardless of service completed) there can be an actuarial increase in the benefits, to take account of the deferment of payment. As a further alternative, benefits could be provided based on any actual salary increases of the member to the date of retirement, or age 70 if earlier. This is the only option open to a 20% director who retires late.

Benefits can be paid at normal pension date, or on actual retirement. A member deferring retirement until after normal pension date may elect to take his or her lump sum benefit at normal pension date and defer the pension. If the member elects to take a pension at normal pension date, the cash payment must be made simultaneously.

13. Employee Contributions

Employees may contribute up to a maximum of 15% of gross pay, provided that the total member contributions do not exceed 5/6ths of the total costs of all benefits being provided. The 15% limit includes voluntary as well as compulsory contributions. Voluntary contributions are permitted on condition that they do not result in the maximum benefit which the Revenue would approve, based on the salary and service of the member, being exceeded.

Special once-off contributions are allowed for tax purposes in the year of payment, if the 15% limit is not exceeded. Where the limit is exceeded, relief on the balance will be spread forward to the member's normal pension date or, if that is not appropriate or possible, back to previous tax years. Any special contributions must be reported in advance to the Revenue Commissioners.

14. Employers' Contributions

Employers' ordinary annual contributions for the cost of providing benefits are fully allowable in the year of payment. A special contribution by the employer would be allowed in the year of payment, to a maximum of (a) £5,000 or (b) the amount of the employer's ordinary annual contributions for pension benefits under all schemes of the employer. Where these limits are exceeded, relief will be spread forward, usually by reference to the amount of the normal or annual contributions each year. Special contributions must always be reported to the Revenue Commissioners.

15 Leaving Service

The Revenue Commissioners do not specify any particular benefits to be granted to the employee, whose rights will be governed by the scheme rules exclusively, except as required by the Pensions Act.. In contributory schemes, contributions which are not the subject of preservation under the Pensions Act may be refunded and these are subject to a tax deduction, currently 25%. The facility to receive a refund of contributions does not apply to 20% Directors whose pensionable salary has at any time exceeded £5,000 per annum. Except where statutory preservation applies, a mixture of deferred benefits and a refund of contributions may not apply except in very restricted circumstances. However, such "mixed" benefits may apply (a) if a statutory benefit is to be preserved but the member wishes to take a refund of pre-1991 contributions; (b) if a transfer payment received from a previous scheme would not be absorbed by a refund - although most transfer payments are now compulsorily preserved by the Pensions Act anyway; (c) if the scheme has switched from a contributory to a non-contributory basis at some time in the past (but not vice versa).

Section A.5:
PUBLIC SECTOR PENSION SCHEMES

Introduction

Public Sector Pension Schemes consist of two broad categories: Statutory Schemes, and Non-statutory Schemes.

Statutory Schemes are those whose operation is governed either by an Act of the Oireachtas, or by Regulations made under a Statutory Instrument in pursuance of such an Act. Examples of these are the Civil Service and Local Government Superannuation Schemes, those of the Defence Forces and the Garda Siochána, and of certain public bodies.

Non-Statutory Schemes apply in most of the Semi-State Bodies, and in a small number of organisations which are part funded by the Exchequer.

Usually, these arrangements consist of two separate schemes: a Superannuation Scheme, which may be contributory or non-contributory; and a Spouses' and Children's Pension Scheme (normally contributory).

Most pension schemes in the public sector are governed by Regulations, which are in most cases issued by the Minister in the sponsoring Department and require the consent of the Minister for Finance. The Superannuation Section of the Department of Finance issues a set of draft Regulations, which outline the standard provisions to be included in such schemes.

Entitlement to benefits under these schemes flows from the Regulations. These may permit the setting up of funded arrangements to secure the benefits, though the schemes covering the majority of public sector employees are unfunded, and operate on a pay-as-you-go basis. If the arrangements are to be funded, then an Exempt Approved Scheme must be set up, whose Rules will reflect the provisions of the Regulations. Such schemes are subject to the normal approval requirements of the 1972 Finance Act. Exceptions to this requirement may occur in certain schemes set up under statutes, which do not need Revenue approval under the 1972 Finance Act, even if they are funded.

The following pages give a broad outline of the pattern of benefits which is usual in the Public Service. There are many exceptions to this pattern, e.g., pension ages differ in the Defence Forces, for Judges and members of the Labour Court, and there are augmentation provisions and special accrual rates for certain types of employee. Schemes set up under local Government arrangements differ in detail from apparently similar schemes in other areas of the public sector. The details given here therefore represent only a broad outline of what is "usual" in the wider public sector.

One principle seems to be common to all schemes - for the most part, augmentation of benefits is not allowed. A power of augmentation exists, but is used extremely sparingly to cater for very special cases, and must be exercised *before* the individual concerned takes up employment.

Almost all schemes in the State sector are exempt from the **Preservation** requirements of the Pensions Act, because their own preservation terms are better. Most funded schemes in the Public Sector have also been exempted from the **Funding Standard** under the Act.

BROAD OUTLINE OF CURRENT PROVISIONS
(PUBLIC SECTOR)

1. ELIGIBILITY: Fulltime permanent employees over age 18, under age 60.

2. NORMAL PENSION DATE: 65th birthday, at which point retirement is usually compulsory.

3. EARLY RETIREMENT:

(a) Normal Health: option to retire is from age 60 onwards;

(b) Ill Health: after 5 years' service. (see also 13.)

Early retirement benefits are based on salary at date of leaving and completed service (plus "added years", if appropriate). There is no reduction for early payment.

4. NORMAL RETIREMENT:

Pension: 1/80th X Final Pensionable Salary X years of service (pro rata for days).

Lump Sum (Gratuity): 3/80ths of Final Salary for each year of service (pro rata for days). May be subject to abatement (see glossary of public sector terminology – Section B2).

Maximum Benefits: 40/80ths of final salary payable in pension form; 120/80ths of salary payable as a gratuity.

Pension Increases: Reviewed in line with salary increases annually, subject to Ministerial approval.

5. BENEFITS ON DEATH
    AFTER RETIREMENT:

Minimum Guaranteed Period of Payment: Nil. The pension ceases on death.

Spouse's Pension: 50% of member's pension.

Children's Pension: 1/3rd of Spouse's pension per dependent child up to a maximum of 3 dependent children.

Pension Increases: As for member's pension.

6. BENEFITS ON DEATH
    BEFORE RETIREMENT:

Lump Sum (Gratuity): 3/80ths of salary for each year of completed service, minimum 1 X salary; maximum 1.5 X salary. May be subject to **abatement** (see glossary).

Spouse's Pension: 50% of member's pension based on projected service to Normal Pension Date.

Children's Pensions: As for death after retirement.

7. INTEGRATION WITH
    SOCIAL WELFARE:

There is a requirement to integrate with Social Welfare for those employees who pay full Pay Related Social Insurance (P.R.S.I.) and, therefore, qualify for a Social Welfare Pension. This is usually arranged by means of salary offset, i.e., Pensionable Salary would be Annual Salary less twice the Social Welfare retirement pension at the rate payable to a single person.

For Gratuity purposes, the full salary is taken into account.

8.	LEAVING SERVICE:	1. If joining another State body, full credit for service may be given by the new employer.

2. If leaving the Public Service with less than 5 years' service, refund of contributions. (But see 14 below).

3. If leaving the Public Service with more than 5 years' service, preserved benefits. These increase during deferment in line with pay for the job.

9.	EMPLOYEES' CONTRIBUTIONS:	Many schemes are non-contributory except for the spouses' and children's benefits. Where employee contributions are paid to the main pension scheme, however, the amounts involved are variable but 5% of pensionable pay is quite common.

10.	PENSIONABLE SERVICE:	Includes all service reckonable under the Local Government (Superannuation) Act, 1956, the Superannuation and Pensions Act, 1963, and any amendment or re-enactment of these. Pensionable service does not have to be continuous.

11.	ILL HEALTH:	Pension and gratuity based on salary and completed service at date of early retirement. Service may be augmented by up to 6.67 years, depending on service actually completed. See also 13.

12. ADDED YEARS:

Members may make additional contributions to purchase additional years of service credit. The Department of Finance Superannuation Section issues tables under which credits of added years and appropriate contribution requirements are calculated.

13. SHORT SERVICE:

If a person leaves through ill health, with less than 5 years' service completed, a gratuity is payable of 1/12th of salary for each year of service. In addition, if completed service is more than 2 years, a further gratuity of 3/80ths of salary for each year is paid.

14. REDUNDANCY:

If a person leaves through redundancy and has no vested rights or transfer entitlement, a refund of contributions with interest is payable.

Section A6:
PUBLIC SERVICE TRANSFER NETWORKS

Public Service transfer networks are vehicles by which employees who work in one part of the public sector, and who transfer to another area of the public sector, can receive full credit for pension purposes with the new employer in respect of service given to the earlier employer. The effect of this is that public sector employees who remain within the broader public service can receive credit for up to 40 years' continuous service for pension purposes, no matter how many times they change their job during their career.

There are two transfer networks in operation.

1. Public Service Network (1979)

This has operated on a provisional basis since 1981 and provides for the reckoning by each participating organisation of earlier pensionable service with any other member of the transfer network. Under its provisions, there is a link between the Civil Service, the Garda Siochána, the Defence Forces, National and Secondary Teachers and over 110 participating bodies, the vast majority of which are in the Public Sector.

Approval of any organisation to participate in this Scheme is looked after by Department of Finance - Superannuation Section. The Scheme is being finalised at present and will be put on a statutory footing in the near future. The Statutory Scheme will be established under Section 3 of the Superannuation and Pensions Act 1976, amending Section 4 of the Superannuation and Pensions Act 1963.

Participating bodies have available to them a number of methods of dealing with transfers. These are set out in full in Paragraph 16 of the draft Scheme, but may be summarised as follows:

A. **"Knock for Knock"** The final Employer pays the total benefits with previous Employers merely confirming the reckonable service with them.

B. The final Employer pays the total benefit when the member retires. Previous Employers pay that employer a contribution to the gratuity payable at the time of retirement and to subsequent payments of pension. What they have to pay is calculated by reference to salary and reckonable service at the time of leaving each previous employer.

1. Pension: 1/80th x reckonable service x salary at leaving.

2. Gratuity: 3/80ths x reckonable service x salary at leaving.

3. Spouses: 50% of members' benefit (for those participating in spouses' and children's pension schemes).

C. As B, but contribution uprated or increased in line with pension increases in the Public Service, i.e. contributions would maintain their value in real terms.

D. A transfer value may be paid at the time of transfer. This is calculated by reference to tables drawn up by the Department of Finance - Superannuation Section. Transfer value is based on full salary in all cases.

Participating bodies have to agree which basis to apply if they each prefer a different option under Paragraph 16 of the draft scheme.

This network covers all transfers from an agreed commencement date, but earlier transfers could be dealt with on a "pre-operative" basis. The final Employer would have to agree to recognise past service not previously transferred, subject to the employee agreeing to pay back any refund or gratuity received, plus interest. The previous Employer could make a contribution but is not obliged to do so.

2. *Local Government Network*

The 1979 draft Network (Public Service) was intended to cater for transfers under both Acts. However, the Department of the Environment took legal advice and, based on this advice, said that it would not participate in the draft Network. In 1984, that Department introduced a separate Network titled "The Local Government (Transfer of Service) Scheme 1984" which brings their transfer provisions into line with the new Network. Bodies wishing to be designated for the purposes of transfer under both the 1956 and 1963 Acts must make separate applications to the appropriate Departments.

The Scheme, as outlined, is similar to the Public Sector Network. A major difference however, is that the contribution system has been confined to "knock for knock" (see A above) or uprated refunds as outlined in C, above..

B

A GLOSSARY OF PENSIONS TERMINOLOGY

Section B1: Occupational Pension Schemes

The purpose of this glossary is to explain as simply as possible a number
of technical terms used in relation to Occupational Pension Schemes. In a
book of this size, it is not possible to cover all the terms used and you
should ask your pension scheme trustees or administrators to explain
anything that you do not understand. A separate glossary of terminology
which tends to be particular to schemes in the State sector appears in
Section B2.

Throughout, any explanation which includes a term or phrase which is
defined elsewhere in the glossaries appears in bold type.

Accrual Rate	The rate at which pension benefit is built up as **pensionable service** is completed in a **defined benefit scheme.** Often expressed as a fraction of **pensionable salary,** e.g., 1/60th for each year of service.
Accrued Benefits	The benefits for service up to a particular point in time, whether **vested rights** or not. These benefits may be calculated in relation to current earnings or projected earnings and allowance might also be made for any increases provided for by the scheme **rules** or by legislation.
Active Member	A member of a pension scheme who is in "reckonable service" – i.e., currently in the employment to which the scheme relates, and who is included in the scheme for a pension benefit.
Actuarial Assumptions	In a **defined benefit scheme** the set of assumptions made by the **actuary** as to rates of return, inflation, increase in earnings, mortality, etc which form the basis of an **actuarial valuation** or other actuarial calculation.

Actuarial Valuation	An investigation by the **actuary** into the ability of a pension scheme to meet its benefit promise. This is usually done to calculate the **recommended contribution rate** which takes account of the actuarial values of **assets** and **liabilities** of the fund. Such an investigation is also needed so that the **actuary** can complete a **funding certificate.**
Actuary	An adviser on financial matters involving the probabilities relating to mortality and other contingencies affecting pension scheme financing. The **Pensions Act** regulates who may function as actuary to a scheme.
Added Years	In private sector schemes this means the provision of extra benefit by adding a period of **pensionable service** in a **defined benefit scheme**. This may arise from the payment into the scheme of a **transfer value**, the payment of **additional voluntary contributions**, or by way of **augmentation**. The term may have different meanings in the context of public sector schemes (see Section B2).
Additional Voluntary Contributions (AVCs)	Contributions made by a **member** over and above his or her normal contributions, if any, in order to secure additional benefits. See Section A3.
Administrator	A person regarded by the **Revenue Commissioners** as responsible for the management of a pension scheme. In a less formal sense it means the person or body which manages the day to day administration of the scheme.

Annual Report	The **Pensions Act** requires the **trustees** of a pension scheme to communicate information about the scheme, its administration and its financial position on a regular basis. The content of the annual report is specified in the **disclosure regulations**. A shorter annual report may be issued for **defined benefit schemes** with fewer than 50 **active members** and for all **defined contribution schemes**.
Annuity	A series of payments made at stated intervals until a particular event - usually the death of the person receiving the annuity - occurs. It is normally secured by the payment of a single premium to an insurance company.
Approved Scheme	An **occupational pension scheme** which is approved by the **Revenue Commissioners** under Chapter II Part I of the Finance Act 1972. See also **Exempt Approved Scheme**.
Assets	The property, investments, debtors, cash and other items of which the **trustees** of a pension scheme are the legal owners.
Augmentation	The term used to describe the provision of additional benefits for or in respect of individual members, where the cost of this provision is borne by the pension scheme itself and/or by the employer.
Average Earnings Scheme	A scheme where the benefit accruing for each year of membership is related to **pensionable earnings** for that year. These schemes are not common.

Beneficiary	A person who is entitled to benefit under a pension scheme, or who will become entitled in specific circumstances (e.g. on the death of a member).
Benefit Statement	A statement of the benefits payable in respect of an individual in certain circumstances, e.g., death, retirement, etc.
Buy-Out	The purchase by the **trustees** of a pension scheme of an insurance policy or bond in the name of a **member** or other **beneficiary** following termination of service, retirement, or on **winding up** of a scheme. The bond is bought in substitution of the member's rights under the pension scheme. Under the **Pensions Act**, purchase of such a bond on leaving service may be at the option of the **member** or, in certain circumstances, at the option of the **trustees**.
Career Average Scheme	An alternative term for an **Average Earnings Scheme**.
Cash Option	An alternative term for **commutation**.
Commutation	An option given to a **member** to replace a series of future payments by an immediate lump sum. The exchange of pension for immediate cash is regulated by the **Revenue Commissioners**. See Section A4.
Commutation Factors	The factors used by the **trustees** to determine the amount of pension which needs to be given up in order to provide a given lump sum benefit.

Concentration of Investment	Placing a significant proportion of the **assets** of a pension scheme in any single investment or category of investments. This is subject to disclosure under the **Pensions Act** and may also impact on the scheme's ability to meet the **funding standard** under the Act.
Continuation Option	A facility offered by an insurance company that insures the death benefits under a scheme, whereby a member leaving the scheme can effect a life policy without evidence of health. Such options are now becoming less common.
Contribution Holiday	A term used to describe a period under which **employers'** and/or **members'** contributions are suspended. This usually happens when the fund is in **surplus.**
Contributory Scheme	A scheme in which **active members** are required to make contributions towards the cost of their benefits.
Corporate Trustee	A company which acts as a **trustee.**
Deed of Appointment	A legal document by which a **trustee** is appointed.
Deferred Annuity	An **annuity** which commences from a future date.
Deferred Benefit	Any benefit whose payment is delayed, e.g., until a person reaches **normal pension age**. Most often used to refer to benefits which accrue to a scheme member on leaving service.
Deferred Pensioner	A person entitled to a pension payment at a future date. Normally this would be an **early leaver** but the term can also be used to describe someone whose retirement has been postponed.

Deferred Retirement	Another term for **late retirement**.
Defined Benefit Scheme	A scheme in which the pension and other benefits which will be paid to the **members** and/or their **dependants** are clearly stated in the **rules** of the scheme. Also known as a **Final Salary Scheme**.
Defined Contribution Scheme	Also known as a **Money Purchase Scheme** - a scheme where the individual **member's** pension is determined solely by reference to the contributions paid into the scheme by or on behalf of that member and the investment return earned on those contributions.
Definitive Trust Deed	The detailed **trust deed** governing a pension scheme which contains details of all the **trustees'** powers. It is usually accompanied by the **rules** of the scheme.
Dependant	A person who is financially dependent on a **member** or **pensioner**, or was so at the time of death or retirement of the **member** or **pensioner**. For **Revenue** purposes, a child of the **member** or **pensioner** may always be regarded as dependent until he or she reaches the age of 18 or ceases to receive full time educational or vocational training if later.
Disability Benefit	A benefit payable to an employee who is unable to work for medical reasons. This may be paid from a pension scheme as an **ill-health early retirement** benefit or it may be payable by the **employer** either directly or under the terms of an insurance policy or **income continuance plan** (which are not part of the pension scheme).

A disability benefit can also arise under a voluntary disability insurance scheme, paid for in full by its **members**. Not to be confused with Social Welfare Disability Benefit.

Disclosure Regulations Regulations issued under the **Pensions Act** requiring disclosure of information about pension schemes and their benefits to interested parties.

Early Leaver A person who ceases to be an **active member** of a pension scheme, other than on death, without being granted an immediate **retirement benefit.**

Early Retirement The retirement of a **member** with immediate benefits, before **normal retirement date**. The benefit may be reduced for early payment. See also **Ill-Health Early Retirement**.

Eligibility The conditions which must be met for a person to be a **member** of a pension scheme or to receive a particular benefit. Eligibility conditions may include provisions relating to age, completion of service, status and type of employment.

Employer The person or body with whom the **member** of a pension scheme has a contract of employment relevant to that scheme.

Equal Access Identical entry conditions for men and women. The **Pensions Act** requires this.

Equal Treatment The principle requiring one sex to be treated no less favourably than the other, as embodied in EC Council Directive 86/378 and the **Pensions Act** (Part VII).

Escalation	A system whereby pensions in payment and/or **preserved benefits** are increased regularly at a fixed or variable percentage rate. The percentage increase applied may be limited to the increase in a specified index. Escalation may be promised and paid for in advance of retirement, or may be granted on a discretionary basis after retirement takes place.
Ex-Gratia Benefit	A benefit provided by the **employer** which it is not legally required to provide. Payment of such a benefit cannot be enforced by the **member**.
Exempt Approved Scheme	An **approved scheme** which is established under **irrevocable trusts**, giving rise to the tax relief allowed for in the Finance Acts.
Final Pensionable Earnings / Final Pensionable Salary	The **pensionable earnings**, at or near retirement or leaving service, on which the pension is calculated. This may be fixed at a particular date or may be based on the average of a number of years.
Final Remuneration	The term used by the **Revenue** for the maximum amount of earnings which it will permit to be used for the purpose of calculating **maximum approvable benefits**. The permissible alternatives are set out fully in the Practice Notes issued by the **Retirement Benefits District** of the **Revenue Commissioners**.
Final Salary Scheme	See **Defined Benefit Scheme**.

Free Cover	The maximum amount of death benefit which an insurance company covering a group of **members** for death benefits is prepared to insure for each individual, without production of evidence of health.
Frozen Benefit	A **preserved benefit**, strictly one which is not subject to **revaluation**.
Funding	The provision in advance for future benefit **liabilities** by setting aside money in a **trust**, which is separate from the **employer's** business, to finance the payment of pensions.
Funding Certificate	A certificate issued by the **actuary** under the **funding standard** provisions of the **Pensions Act**.
Funding Rate	The rate at which contributions are payable to support the liability for benefits. Often used as shorthand for **recommended contribution rate**.
Funding Standard	Provisions under the **Pensions Act**, by which **defined benefit schemes** are subject to periodic **actuarial valuation** and completion of a **funding certificate**, to ensure that their scheme complies with what is termed the funding standard. This is designed to ensure that, at a minimum, the scheme has sufficient funds to secure specified pension rights which **members** have built up, if the scheme should have to be wound up at any stage. Schemes are usually wound up when the **employer** company goes out of business.
Group Policy	An insurance policy issued to cover more than one individual.

Guaranteed Payment Period	A period, normally 5 years, for which payment of a pension will be guaranteed by the scheme rules, whether the **pensioner** lives or dies.
Ill–Health Early Retirement	Retirement on medical grounds before **normal retirement date**. The benefit payable in these circumstances may be greater than that paid to a **member** retiring early in normal health.
Immediate Annuity	An **annuity** which commences immediately, or shortly after, it is purchased.
Income Continuance Plan	One of the terms for **prolonged disability insurance**.
Indexation (also known as Index Linking)	The system under which pensions in payment (and possibly also **preserved benefits**) are increased automatically at regular intervals by reference to the rate of increase in a specified index of prices or earnings.
Individual Arrangement	A pension scheme with only one **member,** whose documents relate only to that **member**.
Inflation Proofing	See **Indexation** and **Escalation**.
Insured Scheme	A pension scheme where the sole long term investment medium used by the **trustees** is an insurance policy (other than a **managed fund** policy).
Integration	The system of designing scheme benefits to take into account all or part of the benefits payable by the state under the social welfare arrangements. Known in public sector schemes as **co-ordination**.

Investment Manager	The person or body to which the investment and management of all or part of the scheme **assets** is delegated by the **trustees**, subject to the provisions of the **trust** documents.
Irrevocable Trust	A **Trust** which cannot be revoked or taken back by the **employer** who establishes it. Such **trusts** are required by the **Revenue Commissioners** in order to give tax free build up to the **assets** of the pension scheme. The **trust** has the effect of separating scheme **assets** from the **assets** of the **employer**, but tax free build up won't be given if there is a possibility that the **employer** could take back the **assets**.
Late Retirement	The retirement of a **member** with immediate payment of benefits, after **normal pension date**.
Liabilities	The obligations of a scheme to pay amounts of money either immediately or in the future. Liabilities whose payment depends on unpredictable future events (such as the death of a **member**) are called "contingent liabilities".
Life Assurance Scheme	A scheme which provides only a benefit payable on the death of a **member**.
Long Service Benefit	A term used under the **Pensions Act** to describe the benefit payable at **normal pension age**.
Managed Fund	An investment contract under which an insurance company offers participation in one or more funds consisting of a collection of pooled **assets**.

Maximum Approvable Benefit	The maximum benefit which the **Revenue Commissioners** will permit to be paid under an **approved scheme** to an individual, taking account of factors such as remuneration and service completed.
Member	A person who has been admitted to membership of a pension scheme and is entitled to benefits under the scheme. This will include **active members**, **pensioners** and **deferred pensioners**.
Member Trustees	**Trustees** who are appointed by **members** or whose appointment by the **employer** has been approved by the scheme **members** in accordance with the regulations made under the **Pensions Act**.
Minimum Retirement Age	The earliest age at which pension scheme **rules** would allow a **member** to retire with an immediate pension, other than on grounds of ill health.
Money Purchase Scheme	Another name for a **defined contribution scheme**.
National Pensions Board	A Board established by the Minister for Social Welfare in 1986 to advise the Minister on pension matters. Not to be confused with the **Pensions Board**.
New Code	A term now practically in disuse to refer to the code of practice relating to the approval of pension schemes by the **Revenue Commissioners** under the 1972 Finance Act.
Nomination	The naming by a **member** of a person or persons to whom he or she wishes any death

benefit to be paid. This will usually not be binding on the **trustees**. Also called a **wishes letter**.

Non-Contributory Scheme	A pension scheme whose rules do not require any contribution from **active members** - i.e., the **employer** is liable for all contributions needed to support the scheme.
Normal Pension Age/ Normal Retirement Age	The age by reference to which the **normal retirement date** is determined.
Normal Pension Date/ Normal Retirement Date	The date at which a **member** of a **pension scheme** normally becomes entitled to receive retirement benefits. This date is the benchmark which determines **early retirement** and **late retirement**.
Occupational Pension Scheme	This is formally defined in the **Pensions Act** as a scheme which is approved under the 1972 Finance Act, or the 1967 Income Tax Act, or whose approval has been applied for to the **Revenue Commissioners**. The term *occupational pension scheme* is generally used to distinguish job related **pension schemes** from state social welfare schemes.
Paid Up Benefit	A benefit secured for an individual **member** under a contract of insurance whose premiums have ceased to be payable in respect of that **member**. One form of **deferred benefit**.
Past Service	Service before a given date (e.g., the date of an actuarial valuation) - frequently used to indicate service before the **member's** entry into the **pension scheme**.

Past Service Benefit	A benefit granted in respect of **past service**.
Pension Fund	Strictly speaking, this is the **assets** of a **pension scheme** but the term is very often used for the scheme itself.
Pension Scheme	An arrangement, other than accident insurance, to provide pension and/or other benefits for **members** on leaving service or retirement and for the **member's dependants** in the event of death.
Pension Plan	Another term for **pension scheme**.
Pensionable Earnings/ Pensionable Salary	The earnings on which benefits and/or contributions are calculated.
Pensionable Service	The period of service which is taken into account in calculating a pension benefit.
Pensioner	A **member** who is currently receiving payment of a pension from a **pension scheme**.
Pensions Act	An Act of 1990 for the regulation of **pension schemes**, which provides for **preservation** of benefits, a **funding standard** in the case of **defined benefit schemes**, **disclosure** of information, equal treatment of men and women, the duties and responsibilities of **trustees** and a **Pensions Board** to supervise the operation of the Act.
Pensions Board	The statutory body set up under the **Pensions Act** to monitor and supervise the operation of the **Pensions Act** and pension developments generally.
Permanent Health Insurance	One of the terms for **prolonged disability insurance**.

Personal Pension Scheme	An alternative method of individual pension provision available in the United Kingdom, but not in Ireland. The term is sometimes also used to describe a **retirement annuity** contract.
Preservation	Describes the obligation which **trustees** have under the **Pensions Act** to retain benefits for scheme **members** who leave the employment and who satisfy certain conditions.
Preserved Benefits	This term is often used to describe any benefit emerging on termination of employment or of membership of a **pension scheme**, which is payable at a later date. Under the **Pensions Act** it has the specific meaning of that part of the benefits which must be preserved as a result of the operation of the Act.
Privately Invested Scheme	A description often applied to a **self-administered scheme**.
Prolonged Disability Insurance	An insurance contract taken out by an **employer** and/or by an employee, designed to pay an income in the event of an employee becoming disabled long term. Benefits under these policies are usually paid after a minimum period of absence from work through illness or injury.
Public Sector Pension Scheme	An **occupational pension scheme** for employees of central or local Government, statutory and other semi-state bodies. Many of these schemes are not funded.
Purchased Life Annuity	An **annuity** purchased privately by an individual **member** is different from the type of annuity purchased by **pension scheme trustees**, which are often described as "compulsory" annuities. In accordance with legislation, part of the

instalment payments of a purchased life annuity are exempt from income tax.

Qualifying Service	A term defined in the **Pensions Act** as the service to be taken into account to entitle a **pension scheme** member to **preserved benefits** on leaving service. Currently it is five years' service, including any period represented by a **transfer value** paid in from another **pension scheme**.
Recommended Contribution Rate	The contribution rate recommended by the **actuary** as being necessary to support the benefit promises made under the scheme.
Retained Benefits	A term used by the **Revenue Commissioners** to denote retirement or death benefits in respect of the earlier service of an employee with a former **employer** or an earlier period of self-employment. These may have to be taken into account in computing **maximum approvable benefits**. (See Section A4).
Retirement Annuity	A contract effected with an insurance company under Sections 235 / 235A of the Income Tax Act 1967. Applicable to the self-employed and to persons in non-pensionable employment. Sometimes called a **personal pension**.
Retirement Benefits District	The branch of the **Revenue Commissioners** which supervises the benefit and contribution structure of **pension schemes** granted approval under the 1972 Finance Act.
Revaluation	The application to **preserved benefits** of compulsory increases in their value prior to the date of payment. Provided for under the **Pensions Act**. This term is often used also to describe any similar non-compulsory increases.

Revenue Commissioners	The organisation charged by Government with the collection of tax revenue and which, through the **Retirement Benefits District**, monitors the operation of **pension schemes** which are granted tax approval.
Rules	The detailed provisions of a **pension scheme**, usually set out in a formal way and given authority by the **trust deed**. They normally accompany the **definitive deed**.
Self-Administered Scheme	A pension scheme where the **assets** are invested, (other than wholly by payment of insurance premiums by the **trustees**), through an in-house manager or an external **investment manager**. The term is not used to indicate the method by which benefits and contributions are administered, but is now almost exclusively used to refer to the way in which the investments are managed.
Self-Investment	The investment of a scheme's **assets** in the business of the **employer** or that of an associated company, or loans made to such bodies out of the pension scheme's **assets**. Regulated under both **disclosure** and **minimum funding standards** provisions of the **Pensions Act**.
State Pensionable Age	The age from which pensions are normally payable by the social welfare scheme, currently 65 (Retirement Pension) or 66 (Old Age Pension) for both men and women.
Surplus	In a **defined benefit scheme**, any excess of the value of a scheme's **assets** over its **liabilities** as calculated by the **actuary** to the scheme. Sometimes referred to as an "actuarial surplus".

Term Assurance Policy	A policy which provides a lump sum on death before a fixed future date. Such policies are frequently used for the provision of lump sum benefits payable on death in service.
Transfer Payment	A payment made from one **pension scheme** to another, or to an insurance company to purchase a **buy-out policy**, in lieu of the benefits which have accrued to the **member** under the scheme. In this form, it specifically refers to transfers made under the **preservation** requirements of the **Pensions Act**. Other payments from one scheme to another are usually called **transfer value**.
Transfer Value	See **transfer payment**.
Trivial Pension	A pension which is so small that it can be subject to full **commutation** without prejudicing the approval of the scheme by the **Revenue Commissioners**. The present triviality limit is £260 per annum.
Trust	A legal concept under which property is held by one or more persons (the **trustees**) for the benefit of other persons (the **beneficiaries**) for the purposes specified by the person setting up the trust. The **trustees** may be **beneficiaries**.
Trust Deed	A legal document, executed in the form of a Deed, which establishes, regulates or amends a **trust**. See **Definitive Trust Deed**.
Trustee	An individual or a company which, alone or jointly, becomes the legal owner of property to be administered for the benefit of someone else (the beneficiaries), in accordance with provisions of the document creating the **trust** and the

provisions of trust law generally and the **Pensions Act**.

Unfunded Scheme	A scheme under which advance financial provision for the payment of benefits is not normally made. Instead the cost of pensions is met from the employer's current income in the same way as the salaries and wages of employees. The term may also be used to describe a scheme where funds are set aside to provide for benefit payments only at the time of a person's retirement.
Valuation Basis	A term commonly used by **actuaries** to mean the method used by them to value the **assets** and **liabilities** of the scheme and the **actuarial assumptions** which they use in this valuation.
Vested Rights	This has different meanings for different people. For **active members**, benefits to which they would unconditionally be entitled on leaving service, which may or may not include statutory rights to **preserved benefits**; For **deferred pensioners** who have already left the employment, their **deferred/preserved benefits**; For **pensioners**, the pension which they are receiving; – including, where appropriate, the related benefits for spouses and other **beneficiaries**.
Wishes Letter	See **nomination**.
Winding Up	The process of terminating a pension scheme, usually by applying the **assets** to the purchase of **immediate** and **deferred annuities** for the **beneficiaries** in accordance with the **trust** document.

65

Abatement	A system under which the **gratuity** payable on retirement or death is reduced by an amount calculated by reference to the period during which a person has not contributed to a **spouses' and children's pension scheme**. Abatement is made even in respect of service before the introduction of such schemes, when it would not have been possible to contribute to them. In practice, abatement at retirement age is treated as a special contribution and relieved from tax.
Added Years	This term has a number of different contexts in the public sector:-

(i) It is sometimes used to indicate **augmentation** of benefits. In general in the public sector, enhancement of benefits without cost to the individual **member** is discouraged but there are limited powers to do it. Such **augmentation** is usually effected by adding a number of notional years of service to the individual's entitlement.

(ii) In the case of early retirement due to ill-health, and sometimes on redundancy, enhancement of an individual's actual service credit by the addition of notional years of service is provided for by **regulations**.

(iii) In cases of **members** whose service to pension age will be short, facilities exist whereby **members** can purchase additional benefits for themselves, either by lump sum purchase, or by regular annual contributions from salary. Whichever way this is done, such enhancement of benefit is also calculated by the addition of notional years of service.

(iv) Professional Added Years - see **Professional Service** below.

Section B2:
PUBLIC SECTOR SCHEMES

Co-Ordination

A term used in the public sector to indicate that the benefits payable under the Social Welfare system are taken into account in the **Occupational Pension Scheme**. See **Integration** in the general Glossary. Co-ordination is generally required as a matter of policy where Social Welfare retirement benefits are payable. However, the calculation of the **gratuity** payable on retirement or death is not normally affected by co-ordination.

Gratuity

A tax free lump sum payment, payable at pension age or on death, which may be subject to **abatement**.

"Knock for Knock"

See **transfer options**.

Marriage Gratuity

A **gratuity** formerly paid to a woman who was obliged to leave service as a result of marriage. Now in disuse.

Parity

A word used to describe the system of increasing pensions in payment and **deferred pensions** in line with the pay for the post held by the scheme **member** before retirement or leaving service, as appropriate.

Pensionable Service

All service reckonable under the local Government (Superannuation Act) 1956, the Superannuation & Pensions Act 1963 and any amendment or re-enactment of these can be included in pensionable service. Pensionable service does not have to be continuous.

Professional Service

A form of "**added years**" awarded in cases where a job specification requires a professional qualification. This service is added to actual service in order to compute eventual pension entitlement and is designed to recognise the time taken to gain the relevant professional qualification.

Regulations	These govern almost every scheme in the public sector and are usually introduced by the Minister in the sponsoring Department and require the consent of the Minister for Finance. They are broadly similar throughout the public sector. Entitlement to benefits under the schemes flows from the regulations. If these permit the setting up of funded arrangements, the funding must be done under an **exempt approved scheme** established in the same way as any private sector scheme and subject to the normal approval requirements of the 1972 Finance Act.
Short Service Gratuity	A **gratuity** paid to a person on leaving service, where the length of **pensionable service** is insufficient to qualify the individual for a **preserved benefit**.
Spouses' and Children's Pension Scheme	A scheme usually separate from the main superannuation scheme in a public sector body, designed to supplement the superannuation scheme and to provide only pensions payable to spouses and children of deceased members. The pensions are payable on death before, or after, retirement. Such schemes are almost always contributory. When these schemes were first introduced, entry was voluntary but became compulsory for subsequent entrants to service.
Statutory Scheme	A scheme whose operation is governed either by an Act of the Oireachtas or by **Regulations** made under a Statutory Instrument in pursuance of such an Act.
Transfer Network	There are two networks in the public service under which the **pensionable service** given in participating bodies can be transferred in full to any other participating body. The two networks

68

involved are the Public Service Transfer Network (1979) and the Local Government (Transfer of Service) Scheme 1984.

Bodies wishing to be designated for the purpose of transfer under both networks must apply separately to the appropriate bodies - the Departments of Finance and Environment respectively.

Transfer Options

Participating bodies have available to them a number of methods of dealing with transfers. They are all subject to the agreement of the old and new employers in each case. They are described in Section A6.

Up-Rating

This is the practice of increasing the value of a benefit or contribution so that it keeps pace with any changes made in the **pensionable pay** appropriate to the job which the person holds or held at a particular time. Up-rating can apply to **deferred benefits**, refunds of contributions which become repayable on re-entry to service and to **marriage gratuities** which are repaid on reinstatement to membership of the scheme.

APPENDIX

Abbreviations commonly found in connection with pension schemes

APLI: Association of Pension Lawyers in Ireland

AVCs: Additional Voluntary Contributions

CAT: Capital Acquisitions Tax

CPI: Consumer Price Index

EC: European Community – Superseded in 1993 by EU.

ECJ: European Court of Justice

EU: European Union

FA: Finance Act

IBA: Irish Brokers Association

IAPF: Irish Association of Pension Funds

IBEC: Irish Business & Employers Confederation

ICTU: Irish Congress of Trade Unions

IIF: Irish Insurance Federation

IIPM: Irish Institute of Pensions Managers

ITA: Income Tax Act

NPA: Normal Pension Age

NPD: Normal Pension Date

NRA: Normal Retirement Age

NRD: Normal Retirement Date

NPB: National Pensions Board

OPAS: Occupational Pensions Advisory Service (United Kingdom)

OPB: Occupational Pensions Board (United Kingdom)

PAYE: Pay as you Earn

PDI: Prolonged Disability Insurance

PHI: Permanent Health Insurance

PLA: Purchased Life Annuity

PMI: The Pensions Management Institute

PPP: Personal Pension Plan

PSO: Pension Schemes Office (United Kingdom)

PUP: Paid Up Pension (ie., deferred pension)

RPCI: Retirement Planning Council of Ireland

SORP: Statement of Recommended Practice

SSAP: Statement of Standard Accounting Practice

SSAS: Small Self-Administered Scheme

TLA: Term Life Assurance, or Temporary Life Assurance

T/V: Transfer Value